ACCOUNTABILITY

A Guide to Accountability-Based Management

Ginty Burns

Note for Librarians: A cataloguing record for this book is available from Library and Archives Canada at www.collectionscanada.ca/amicus/index-e.html
ISBN 1-4120-6560-7

Printed in Victoria, BC, Canada. Printed on paper with minimum 30% recycled fibre. Trafford's print shop runs on "green energy" from solar, wind and other environmentally-friendly power sources.

Offices in Canada, USA, Ireland and UK
This book was published *on-demand* in cooperation with Trafford Publishing. On-demand publishing is a unique process and service of making a book available for retail sale to the public taking advantage of on-demand manufacturing and Internet marketing. On-demand publishing includes promotions, retail sales, manufacturing, order fulfilment, accounting and collecting royalties on behalf of the author.

Book sales for North America and international:
Trafford Publishing, 6E–2333 Government St.,
Victoria, BC v8t 4p4 CANADA
phone 250 383 6864 (toll-free 1 888 232 4444)
fax 250 383 6804; email to orders@trafford.com
Book sales in Europe:
Trafford Publishing (uk) Ltd., Enterprise House, Wistaston Road Business Centre,
Wistaston Road, Crewe, Cheshire cw2 7rp UNITED KINGDOM
phone 01270 251 396 (local rate 0845 230 9601)
facsimile 01270 254 983; orders.uk@trafford.com
Order online at:
trafford.com/05-1471

10 9 8 7 6 5 4 3 2

What this book is for

This book is a quick and easy reference on the concepts of accountability-based management. You can use it to learn about and apply the principles in your workplace, or to refresh your memory if things seem to be going off the rails.

Who this book is for

Anyone in a business organization who is interested in building a trust-enhancing workplace where people have fulfilling work, are treated fairly, and can count on their manager to add value.

Acknowledgements

Elliott Jaques, for the foundational work on requisite organization.

My colleagues at COREinternational for their support and contributions.

John Bryan (Toronto, ON) for his work on the six levels of participation in decision-making.

Matthew Allen (Toronto, ON) for original artwork.

William Bushell (Victoria, BC) for graphics and cover design.

Web resources

Word definitions: Merriam-Webster Online (www.m-w.com)

Quotations: The Quotations Page (www.quotationspage.com) and Bartleby Books Online (www.bartleby.com)

Biographical information: A&E Television Networks (www.biography.com)

Contents

Preface

This book describes how things should work in an organization that uses accountability-based principles. People often say, "But what is an accountability-based company, and how do I know when I've got one?" Well, there are some indicators. It's unlikely all of these will be true, but if most of them are, you are almost there. In an accountability-based company...

- everyone experiences their role as challenging, allowing them to exercise their creative potential within appropriate boundaries.

- everyone can count on their various vertical and horizontal role relationships to help get their work done by providing what is needed in a timely way.

- managers are called to account not only for their team's results but also for their effectiveness as managerial leaders.

- reward and recognition systems (e.g. compensation, performance evaluation) support the organization's values, business strategy and structure principles.

- change management and organization design are based on principles, not driven by personality, power, or influence.

- everyone can focus on their work because they can trust others to do theirs.

- everyone knows what's expected of them and by when.

- there is timely and factual feedback on personal effectiveness.

- everyone can see how they contribute to the organization's goals.

- everyone lives the organization's values.

- there are the right number of management layers.

- every role and level is understood as important and required for success.

- people fit their roles perfectly.

- everyone's accountability is fully matched with authority.

- decisions occur at the right organizational layer.

- work is grouped in a way that minimizes coordination cost, reduces escalation, and eliminates dysfunctional boundary management.

- managers support their direct reports, but don't do their work or tell them how to do it.

- there is fair, non-arbitrary evaluation of everyone's contribution.

- everyone has someone accountable for their development—their manager's manager.

- there is career mentoring for all, not just a select few.

- people feel they are paid fairly.

- there is a belief that everyone is "doing their best."

A is for accountability

Accountable (adj):	subject to giving an account
Account (n):	a statement explaining one's conduct; a statement or exposition of reasons, causes, or motives

Accountability is not the same as responsibility, which is a felt obligation to act within an organization's values (see *Responsibility*, page 70.) Being accountable means you can be called to answer for your own actions and, if you are a manager, for the outputs of your direct reports. The notion of a manager being accountable for his/her direct reports' outputs may seem odd at first, but is logical when you consider that a manager determines the goals for those direct reports, monitors their work, and provides the resources they need to do their work.

In an accountability-based company...

• People understand what they and others are accountable for.

• People get called to account if they do not meet expectations—there are consequences.

"It is not only what we do, but also what we do not do for which we are accountable." (Molière, French actor and comic dramatist, 1622–1673)

Here's what ALL EMPLOYEES are accountable for at all times:

- Doing their best
- Supporting company values and goals
- Working cooperatively with others
- Carrying out assigned work
- Informing their manager if progress on tasks is better or worse than expected
- When in doubt, asking their manager to clarify expectations

MANAGERS are also accountable for the following:

- The work their direct reports produce
- The result or impact of their direct reports' behaviour
- Building and sustaining an effective team capable of producing required outputs
- Continually improving processes
- Providing their team with effective managerial leadership, which includes
  - holding regular team meetings
  - setting context for work
  - planning
  - assigning work effectively
  - appraising team members' personal effectiveness
  - carrying out merit reviews
  - coaching
  - selecting and inducting team members
  - when appropriate, deselecting a team members from roles

And MANAGERS-ONCE-REMOVED (people who manage managers) are also accountable for the following:

- Ensuring their direct reports exercise sound managerial leadership practices
- Establishing work levels and placement in compensation bands for employees-once-removed (employees two levels down, or EoRs)
- Developing a talent pool of EoRs (includes mentoring and career planning)
- Assessing their EoRs' current capability
- Planning succession for roles one level down
- Ensuring EoRs are treated fairly and equitably across the organization
- Finalizing their EoRs' placement in/removal from role and, when appropriate, removal from the organization
- Ensuring their EoRs are able to maintain effective cross-boundary relationships

B is for boundaries

Boundary (n): something (as a line, point, or plane) that indicates or fixes a limit or extent

We all live and work within social, legal, and organizational boundaries. Some boundaries are narrow and restrictive, while some are wide. In an organization, it's important to know where the boundaries of your role are—what you can do yourself and what you have to go to others for. Knowing the boundaries and having the authority to act within them is empowering rather than restrictive.

In an accountability-based company...

- Managers work with their direct reports to clearly define what the direct reports can and cannot do.

- People understand their own and others' boundaries and decision-making authorities.

- Managers encourage their direct reports to exercise discretion and creativity within the defined boundaries.

- Boundaries are wide enough to allow people to do their work effectively.

"Freedom is not the absence of structure... but rather a clear structure that enables people to work within established boundaries in an autonomous and creative way." (Erich Fromm, German psychologist and social philosopher, 1900–1980)

C is for capability

Capable (adj):   having attributes (as physical or mental power) required for performance or accomplishment

Each person's capability to do work grows over time until it reaches the maximum potential for that person. Someone placed in a job for which he/she is under- or over-capable at a particular time will be dissatisfied and may fail, so it's important to match capability to the job requirements. (See also *Information processing capability*, page 37 and *Level of work complexity*, page 48)

A manager-once-removed (someone who manages managers) is accountable to assess the capability of employees two levels down, ensure a proper fit of people to roles, and see that people have opportunities to grow into more complex roles as they develop.

There are three types of capability:

Current applied capability   the level of work a person is capable of doing right now

Current potential capability   the level of work a person would be capable of doing right now if he/she had some training or a little more experience

Future potential capability   the maximum level of work a person will be able to perform in future

In an accountability-based company...

- There is a good match between an individual's capability and the complexity of work in that person's role.

- Managers ensure direct reports have the knowledge and skills to perform effectively in their roles.

- Managers-once-removed are aware of the current and future potential capability of employees two levels down and provide appropriate career development and mentoring to help them reach their potential.

Assessing current applied or current potential capability is not a complicated procedure involving testing and allocation of points. It is a judgment call, where a manager-once-removed and manager review how someone is performing in a particular role by asking these questions:

- Is this person able to do the work of this role right now?

- Would this person be able to do work at the next level up right now? If not now, when?

- How does this person compare to others in similar roles?

- Does this person solve problems in an appropriate way?

- Does this person do work that, while good, is more than required within the role? (an indicator of over-capability)

"If your tools are less than what you need, you will expend effort unnecessarily. If they are more than what you need, you will over-invest money, time, and attention to acquire and maintain something that's not worth the effort." (David Allen, American consultant, trainer, and author, 1945–)

C is also for coaching

Coach (v):   to train intensively (as by instruction and demonstration)

Coaching is an important part of a manager's job. It involves helping direct reports do their current work faster and more easily. Everyone is entitled to coaching from his/her manager, but no-one is obliged to receive it if it's not needed. Since coaching is related to current work only, it is different from mentoring and career development, both of which are the accountability of a manager-once-removed (see page 53).

In an accountability-based company...

- Managers find out what coaching their direct reports need and provide it at the right time.

- People feel comfortable asking their manager for coaching.

- Managers-once-removed ensure their employees-once-removed receive appropriate coaching from their manager.

"A good coach will make his players see what they can be rather than what they are." (Ara Parasheghian, American football coach)

And C is for collateral teams

Collateral (adj):   serving to support or reinforce; parallel, coordinate, or corresponding in position, order, time, or significance

A collateral team is a team of people who report to the same manager.

To ensure effective teamwork, it's important for collateral team members to

- differentiate their work as a team from their work as individual team members.

- understand when the team needs to meet, and when the manager needs to be present, in order to get work done effectively.

- manage their relationships so they work well together.

In an accountability-based company…

- Collateral team members share their manager's concern for the overall effectiveness of his/her area.

- Individual team members do what's right for the team and the company as a whole, not just what's right for themselves or their own functional area.

- If in conflict, individual team members think "what would my manager want me/us to do for the good of the team?"

"What we need to do is learn to work in the system, by which I mean that everybody, every team, every platform, every division, every component is there not for individual competitive profit or recognition, but for contribution to the system as a whole on a win-win basis." (W. Edwards Deming, American statistician and management consultant, 1900–1993)

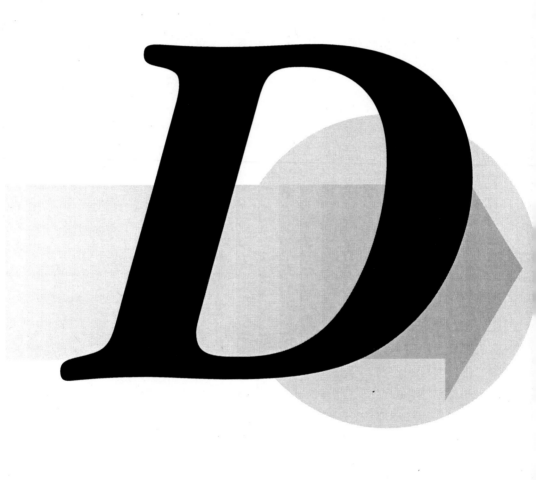

D is for decision-making authority

Decision (n):   a determination arrived at after consideration

Authority (n):   power to influence or command thought, opinion,
                       or behaviour

Decision-making authority is one of the resources a manager grants
to a direct report, and it forms one of a role's boundaries.
Understanding what level of decision-making authority someone has
been granted helps to reduce unnecessary meetings and conflict.
There are six levels of involvement in decision-making:

Be aware   to be informed of a decision before it's implemented

Contribute   to be asked for input before a decision is made

Participate   to participate in discussions before a decision is made

Recommend   to recommend what a decision should be

Decide   to have the authority to decide

Veto   to have veto power over a decision

In an accountability-based company...

- People know who makes which decisions.

- People have sufficient decision-making authority to carry out
  their work.

- When people meet to make a decision, those with the authority
  to do so are in the room.

- People know when a decision must be escalated, and why.

- People understand the degree of influence they have over
  decisions others make.

"Nothing is more difficult, and therefore more precious, than to be able to decide."
(Napoleon Bonaparte, French general, consul, and emperor, 1769–1821)

D is also for delegating work

Delegate (v):   to entrust to another; to appoint as one's representative; to assign responsibility or authority

Because the President or CEO of a company cannot do all the work alone, he/she sets up direct report roles and delegates portions of work. Those roles in turn set up other roles, and so on down to the front line. But what work to delegate, and what to keep? It's important to make sure that each role holder is capable of, and doing, work at the right level (see *Level of work complexity,* page 48). Typically a President in an organization with five layers of work complexity will be doing level 5 work, with a longest task of 5–10 years. However, not all the President's work will be of this duration—there will be other, shorter-term work that the President must do him/herself, such as giving Board presentations, and providing managerial oversight to direct reports. The President can delegate portions of work (with appropriate timespans) to direct reports, but he/she should never delegate the level 5 work: that is abdication! The same is true all the way down the accountability hierarchy.

Some guidelines for delegating work:

- Delegate as much as possible, as long as the delegated work falls within the work level and capability of your direct report.

- Set appropriate context for the delegated work.

- Decide if the work output must come back to you once it's completed.

- Be clear about the quantity, quality, time, and resources for delegated work (See *QQTR*, page 66).

- Make sure the direct report understands and commits to doing the work.

- Don't delegate your own managerial accountabilities (see *Accountability*, page 2).

In an accountability-based company...

- People understand what their own work is and what they can delegate.

- Managers delegate work clearly, being specific about why it needs to be done, how, with what, and by when.

- People let their manager know if they are unable to take on delegated work—and what would need to change for them to be able to do it.

- Managers don't duplicate work they have delegated to someone else.

- Managers never delegate their managerial leadership practices (see *Manager*, page 52).

To ensure delegated work is at the right level of complexity for a direct report, ask yourself these questions:

- How long will I give the person to do this task?

- If pressed, would I give the person any longer? What's the longest I could live with?

- Are there stages along the way, where I need to sign off on something before the work can proceed? When would they be?

Then make sure the answer fits with the role's designated level of work complexity:

Level 1 (0–3 months)
Level 2 (3–12 months)
Level 3 (1–2 years)
Level 4 (2–5 years)
Level 5 (5–10 years)

"No man will make a great leader who wants to do it all himself or get all the credit." (Andrew Carnegie, Scottish industrialist and philanthropist, 1835–1919)

E is for employees and employees-once-removed

Employee (n):   one employed by another, usually for wages or salary

Employ (v):   to make use of (someone or something inactive); to use advantageously; to use or engage the services of; to provide with a job that pays wages or a salary

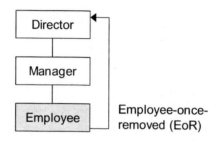

Without employees, companies could not function. Through people, organizations achieve their mandate and make their contributions to society. Since people come to work for many reasons—financial, social, and personal satisfaction—a company will likely benefit from providing meaningful, rewarding work for people at fair rates of pay, in a trust-enhancing environment. Under these circumstances, employees can be expected to do their best (and can be called to account for not doing so).

Whatever your title (Associate, Team Member, Vice President...) if you receive pay for working in an organization, you are an employee accountable for doing your best always. As an employee, you can count on your manager to provide effective managerial leadership, which includes setting context for work, assigning work effectively, appraising your personal effectiveness, carrying out merit reviews, and coaching.

If your manager has a manager, you are that person's employee-once-removed and you can count on your manager-once-removed to ensure you are fairly treated and fairly paid, and help you with career planning if required. (See also *Accountability,* page 2, *Manager,* page 52, *Manager-once-removed,* page 53, and *Three-tier units,* page 82.)

In an accountability-based company...

- Employees feel fairly paid for the work they do.

- Employees feel fairly treated or, if not, can appeal to their manager or manager-once-removed.

- Employees-once-removed have access to their manager-once-removed for career planning.

- Employees experience trust and know that no-one will intentionally do them harm.

- Employees understand and support the company's values.

- All employees, at every level, are valued.

"Most are engaged in business the greater part of their lives, because the soul abhors a vacuum and they have not discovered any continuous employment for man's nobler faculties." (Henry David Thoreau, American writer and poet, 1817–1862)

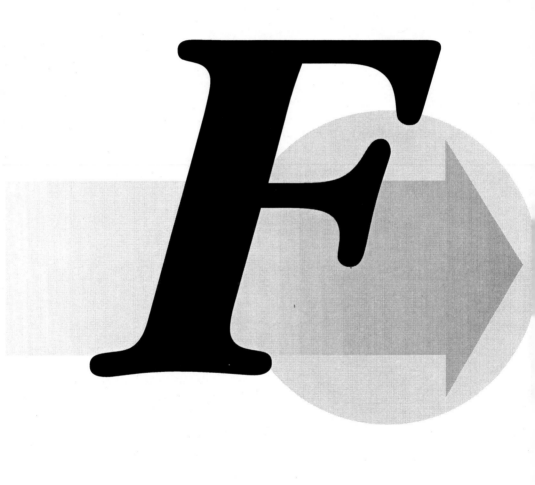

F is for felt-fair pay

Feel (v):   to undergo passive experience of; to have one's sensibilities
                       markedly affected by; to be aware of by instinct or inference

Fair (adj):   pleasing to the eye or mind; marked by impartiality and
                       honesty; free from self-interest, prejudice, or favouritism;
                       conforming with the established rules; sufficient but
                       not ample

Pay (n):   something paid for a purpose and especially as a salary
                       or wage

Most people want to be paid fairly for the work they do, and to feel others within their organization are also paid fairly. The best way to promote fairness is for a company to have pay bands that match the levels of work complexity—in other words, pay is based on the complexity of work in a role as opposed to the individual who is doing the work. And as long as the individual fits the role well in terms of having the right information processing capability, possessing appropriate knowledge and skills, and valuing the work, the pay will be seen as fair.

While some organizations try to place people in pay bands through an "objective" points system, the level of pay for a role is, in fact, a judgment that a role's manager and manager-once-removed make. The final decision on pay must be made in the context of discussions with other managers/managers-once-removed and HR representatives, and within a company's established compensation system.

In an accountability-based company...

- Pay bands line up with the organization's levels of work.

- People feel fairly paid for the work they do.

- Managers recommend pay levels for their direct reports.

- Managers-once-removed meet with their own direct reports to discuss the effects of pay changes for employees-once-removed within the three-tier unit (see page 82).

- Groups of managers-once-removed (with HR representatives) discuss pay bands and agree on fair and equitable pay for their employees-once-removed within broad company compensation guidelines.

- There is openness about pay bands and about reasons for anomalies.

- People understand that pay takes into account skill scarcity and other temporary market conditions, but the environment is constantly under review and adjustments made as things change.

"It is not wealth one asks for, but just enough to preserve one's dignity, to work unhampered, to be generous, frank, and independent." (W. Somerset Maugham, English dramatist and novelist, 1874–1965)

F is also for form follows function

Form (n):   the shape and structure of something as distinguished from its material

Function (n): the action for which a person or thing is specially fitted or used, or for which a thing exists

A company's structure needs to be designed so the company can most effectively achieve its strategy. This involves having the right number of layers of management, and the right types of work taking place in the right groups. Failure to pay attention to how work is grouped and layered wastes effort, time, and money.

In an accountability-based company...

- There are exactly the right number of management layers, with effective distribution of accountability and authority.

- Work is grouped to minimize cross-boundary friction and coordination costs.

- If the strategy (the function) changes, senior managers automatically review the organization's structure (the form).

"The structures that we create and use must match their intended purpose—no more and no less—to be the most effective." (David Allen, American management consultant, trainer, and author)

G is for gap

Gap (n):   a separation in space; an incomplete or deficient area

Whatever a role's level of work complexity (see *Level of work complexity*, page 48), the role-holder's manager should be capable of, and working at, one level higher. If a manager is working more than one level above, it causes a gap. Someone who is in a gap with his/her manager might say,

> "My manager appears to have his head in the clouds and doesn't appreciate the issues I have to deal with in my work."

> "I often have to do my manager's job, and it's a real struggle—I don't think I do it very well."

While the manager in a gap situation might say,

> "I have to spend an inordinate amount of time explaining things to my direct report, who still doesn't understand the needs well enough."

> "I feel like I'm always being pulled down into the weeds rather than concentrating on what really matters."

In an accountability-based company...

- Each employee has a manager capable of doing work exactly one level higher in complexity.

- Gaps are not built into the structure (except perhaps temporarily, with careful thought and awareness of how to manage the gap).

Note: It can be OK for an individual contributor to be in a gap situation with his/her manager, particularly if the role provides direct output support to that manager (see *Output*, page 58 and *Individual contributors,* page 36).

"Every one of us gets through the tough times because somebody is there, standing in the gap to close it for us." (Oprah Winfrey, American actress and television talk show host, 1954–)

G is also for goals

Goal (n): the end toward which effort is directed

We need goals if we are not to wander aimlessly through work and life. In an organization, people need to understand what the strategy is and how their work fits into that strategy. People are usually more effective if they know why they are doing things—how achieving their goals helps their manager achieve his/hers, and so on right up to the top layers of the company.

Although managers determine their direct reports' overall goals, managers and direct reports should work together to flesh out the details of how the goals will be achieved. Managers also need to make sure that the overall goals fit within the timespan of a direct report's level of work (see *Level of work complexity*, page 48).

There are various other terms for a goal—objectives, key performance indicators (KPIs), key results areas (KRAs)... the terminology is less important than ensuring people are set up for success by matching goals to the level of work complexity in a role.

In other words...

For this level of role	The longest goal is
1	3 months
2	1 year
3	2 years
4	5 years
5	10 years

In an accountability-based company...

- All employees understand the company's strategy.

- All employees have clearly defined goals with timespans that are appropriate for their role.

- Everyone understands how his/her own goals help the company achieve its strategy.

- People are evaluated not just on whether or not they achieved their goals, but under what conditions and how they did it.

"Without goals and plans to reach them, you are like a ship that has set sail with no destination." (Fitzhugh Dodson, American psychologist and author, 1923–)

H is for hierarchy

Hierarchy (n):   a division of angels; the classification of a group of people according to ability or to economic, social, or professional standing

The majority of people in North America work in a hierarchical organization. To some, the word hierarchy denotes bureaucracy and power—things that stifle creativity and initiative. However, an accountability-based hierarchy is not about power. Instead, it's a way of ensuring the right people are doing the work the company needs to get done, people have clear roles and appropriate authority to act, and each managerial layer adds value.

In an accountability-based company...

- There are just the right number of layers of management—not too many, not too few.

- People know who is accountable for the work they do, and who to go to when they have problems.

- People know what their own work is, and what their boundaries are.

"Every seeming equality conceals a hierarchy." (Mason Cooley, American aphorist, 1927–)

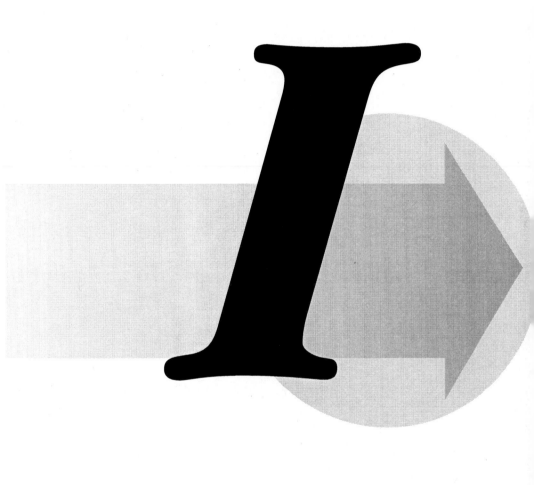

I is for individual contributors

Individual (n):   a particular being or thing as distinguished from a class, species, or collection. (Obsolete meaning: inseparable)

Contributor (n):   one who gives or supplies in common with others; one who plays a significant part in bringing about an end or result

Individual contributors are people who provide specialized knowledge or skills, such as a legal advisor or IT expert. They usually don't have direct reports, but this doesn't mean they perform only level 1 work (see *Level of work complexity*, page 48). An individual contributor can work at any level in an organization, and can do work that supports roles working up to two levels above or below that of his/her own.

In an accountability-based company...

- Individual contributors are recognized and valued for the work they do.

- Individual contributors are not required to manage people to obtain pay or status increases.

"To a specialist, his specialty is the whole of everything and if his specialty is in good order, and it generally is, then everything must be succeeding." (Gertrude Stein, American author, 1874–1946)

I is also for information processing capability (IPC)

Information (n):   the communication or reception of knowledge or intelligence

Process (v):   to subject to examination or analysis

Work involves thinking (see *Work,* page 94), and whenever people work they are processing information to make decisions. As work becomes more complex, there are more pieces of information to consider, and more chance that changing one thing could affect many others. How an individual processes information indicates what level of work he/she is most suited for. For example, a person who is most happy making straight choices within guidelines is probably best suited to level 1 work (see *Level of work complexity,* page 48), while a person who likes to explore multiple avenues and consider "well, if I did this, then that might happen and on the other hand if I did this then that might happen…" is likely best suited to level 4 work. Matching information processing capability to the level work in a role is important: a level 1 sales clerk who explores multiple options and "what ifs" before making a decision on a simple customer complaint is unlikely to satisfy the customer's needs in a timely manner!

Note: information processing capability is not something people can improve through training. Everyone develops at his/her own speed to a maximum level that is different for each person. (See also *Capability,* page 8 and *Role-person fit,* page 72.)

In an accountability-based company…

- People have the right information processing capability for the work they need to do.

- Managers' information processing capability is one level higher than that of their direct reports.

"Thinking is the hardest work there is, which is why so few managers engage in it." (Henry Ford, American automobile industrialist, 1863–1947)

And I is for interdependence

Interdependent (adj): mutually dependent

Dependent (adj): determined or conditioned by another; relying on another for support

In most companies, groups and role-holders depend on each other's outputs to meet their own business goals (see also *Cross-boundary relationships,* page 98). There are three different degrees of interdependence[1]:

Pooled
There is little interaction between groups, but all groups must work effectively to meet overall business goals. (Such groups do not need to be under a common manager.)

Sequential
There is a handoff from one group to the next, where the work outputs of the first group become the inputs of the next. (Such groups may or may not be under a common manager.)

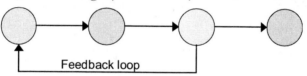
Feedback loop

Reciprocal
The work outputs of one group immediately affect the other group, and vice versa. Each unit's work is contingent on the work of the other, requiring constant mutual adjustment. (Such groups should be organized under a common manager as low as possible in the organization hierarchy.)

---

[1] As defined by James D. Thompson in his book *Organizations in Action,* New York: McGraw Hill, 1967

Grouping highly (reciprocally) interdependent processes or groups under a common manager minimizes cross-functional barriers and focuses the groups on the same priorities, allowing the group members to more effectively meet their goals.

In an accountability-based company...

- Work is grouped appropriately to minimize cross-functional friction and promote goal achievement.

- Different groups understand how each contributes to the other, and why it's necessary to work collaboratively.

- If problems arise, people understand who they need to talk to and can determine when escalation is required.

"It is a good thing to be dependent on each other for something: it makes us civil and peaceable." (Sojourner Truth, American Abolitionist and women's rights activist, c.1797–1883)

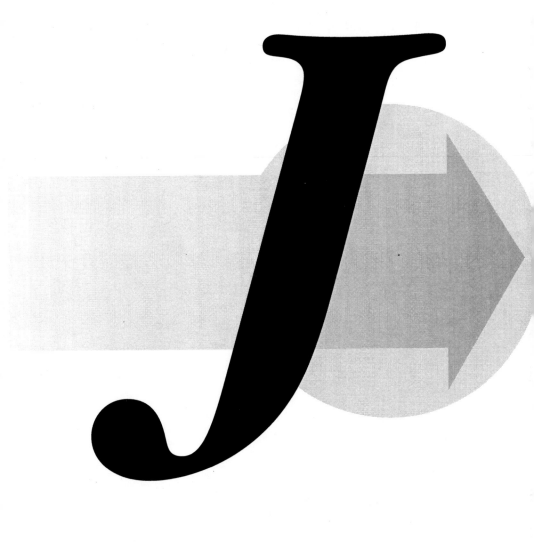

J is for jam-up

Jam (v):   to become blocked or wedged; to become unworkable through the jamming of a movable part; to make unintelligible by sending out interfering signals or messages

If someone is performing work at the same level of complexity as his/her manager, they are both probably experiencing a jam-up. A direct report in a jam-up with his/her manager might say,

> "My manager is always interfering and won't leave me alone to get on with my work."

> "My manager doesn't set appropriate context for my work—I usually go elsewhere for this."

> "My manager and I work more like colleagues than roles in a reporting relationship."

> "My manager and I both do the same things, so work gets duplicated."

And a manager experiencing a jam-up with his/her direct reports might say,

> "I share my work with my employees as equal partners. It helps keep them motivated, although it does make my job less challenging."

> "There's a lot of work I could delegate but I don't, because I don't want my direct reports to get all the interesting stuff even though they keep asking for it."

In an accountability-based company…

- Each employee has a manager capable of doing, and performing, work exactly one level higher in complexity.

- Jam-ups are not built into the structure (except perhaps temporarily, with careful thought and awareness of how to manage the jam-up).

Note: It can be OK for an individual contributor (a role with no direct reports who provides specialized knowledge or skills) to be in a jam-up situation with his/her manager.

"The best executive is the one who has sense enough to pick good men to do what he wants done, and the self-restraint to keep from meddling with them while they do it." (Theodore Roosevelt, 26th US President, 1858–1919)

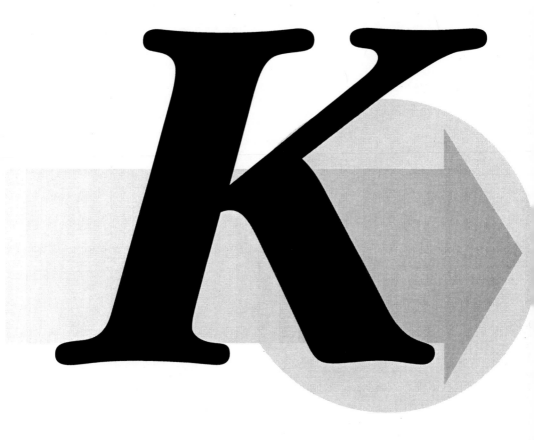

K is for knowledge

Knowledge (n):   the fact or condition of knowing something with familiarity gained through experience or association

To do a job well, you need appropriate knowledge, which is something you gain from education and experience. While a manager ensures his/her direct reports receive appropriate coaching to do their current work, a manager-once-removed ensures employees two levels down get opportunities to gain knowledge for career development.

In an accountability-based company...

- Managers are aware of what coaching their direct reports need, and see that they get it.

- Managers-once-removed work with their employees-once-removed to develop career plans, and provide opportunities to help employees-once-removed achieve their goals.

"It is possible to fly without motors, but not without knowledge and skill."
(Wilbur Wright, American airplane designer and aviation pioneer, 1867–1912)

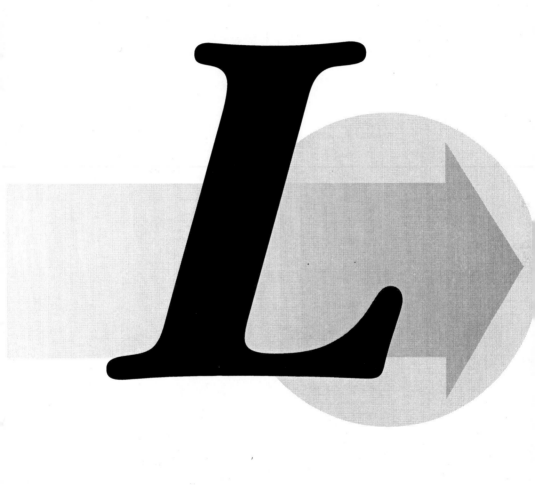

L is for level of work complexity

Level (n):   a position in a scale

Work (n):   activity in which one exerts strength or faculties to do or perform something; sustained physical or mental effort to overcome obstacles and achieve an objective or result

Complex (adj):   composed of two or more parts

In every company there is work to be done. Some of it is complex, some of it is simple, and all of it is important.

The principle of level of work complexity (LW) is based on research done over many years by Elliott Jaques (1917-2003) and described in his book *Requisite Organization.* Jaques determined that work is a thinking process that involves using judgment and making decisions to achieve a result or *output*, and discovered seven layers (strata) of work complexity within organizations.

Jaques also found that the way of measuring work complexity was to measure the longest task assigned to a role (the role's *timespan of discretion*, see page 84*).* His theory was that the longer a manager gave a role-holder to do a certain task, the more other things that person had to juggle and balance to get everything done at the right time, and therefore the more complex the role's work.

Not all organizations have seven layers of work complexity. A small family-owned business might have two. A medium-sized business or a profit-and-loss unit of a larger organization usually has five. Most world-wide corporations have seven. In his later life, Jaques identified some super-corporations with eight levels of work complexity.

The following diagram gives an example of the type of work and longest task timespans for the seven levels of work complexity.

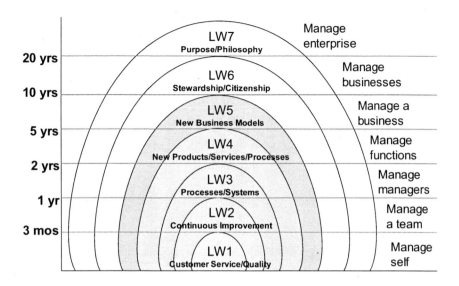

	LW7 Purpose/Philosophy	Manage enterprise
20 yrs	LW6 Stewardship/Citizenship	Manage businesses
10 yrs	LW5 New Business Models	Manage a business
5 yrs	LW4 New Products/Services/Processes	Manage functions
2 yrs	LW3 Processes/Systems	Manage managers
1 yr	LW2 Continuous Improvement	Manage a team
3 mos	LW1 Customer Service/Quality	Manage self

Notes:

- While timespan of longest task is the only objective way to measure work complexity, there are other indicators, such as having a larger number of variables to deal with.

- Whether or not you have direct reports does not determine level of work complexity. Individual contributors could be at any level in an organization, and there are some companies where front-line work is level 2.

In an accountability-based company...

- People understand how many levels of work are required to achieve the company's strategy.

- People understand what distinguishes the different levels.

- Each level of work is staffed with people capable of working at that level.

- Each level of work is valued.

"There are no menial jobs, only menial attitudes." (William Bennett, American federal official and author, 1943–)

M is for manager

Manager (n):   a person who conducts business or household affairs; a person whose work or profession is management; a person who directs a team or athlete

Management (n):   the conducting or supervising of something (as a business)

Managers meet their goals through a combination of their own work and that of their direct reports. Since managers are accountable for the work direct reports produce (their results), and the impacts of direct reports' behaviour, they need to be able to develop and lead effective teams. (See also *Three-tier units*, page 82.)

In an accountability-based company...

- Each employee has a manager capable of doing work exactly one level higher in complexity.

- Managers are held to account for whether or not their direct reports achieve their goals and required results, and for how they did their work.

- Managers carry out the following managerial leadership practices, and are evaluated on how well they do them:

  - holding regular team meetings.

  - setting context for direct reports' work.

  - planning their own and their department's work.

  - assigning work clearly.

  - appraising direct reports' personal effectiveness.

  - carrying out merit reviews.

  - providing coaching for direct reports.

  - selecting and inducting team members.

  - when appropriate, deselecting team members from role.

  - continually improving processes.

- There are consequences for managers who don't perform their managerial leadership practices effectively.

"Management is doing things right; leadership is doing the right things."
(Peter Drucker, Austrian-born writer and management consultant, 1909–)

M is also for manager-once-removed

Removed (adj):   distant in degree of relationship

Your manager-once-removed (MoR) is your manager's manager—sometimes called a *skip-level manager*—and you are that person's employee-once-removed (EoR). If you have direct reports who manage people, you are the manager-

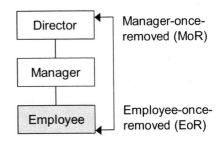

once-removed to those people, and they are your employees-once-removed. An MoR has accountabilities that differ from those of a manager (see *Accountability, page 2)*. It is the MoR's job to manage the talent pool, ensure EoRs are paid fairly and equitably, provide mentoring to EoRs, and ensure there are successors for key roles. MoRs must also make sure their own direct reports are effective managers.

Groups of MoRs need to meet at least once a year to discuss their EoRs' level of work and pay bands, and identify development opportunities for EoRs.

If you are an MoR, this means you have to know all your EoRs, at least visually and preferably by name. You will need to know who they are, where they work, their important career aspirations, how they're doing, and their potential for promotion. Your direct reports (your EoRs' managers) can help you with this. You don't have to meet with each of your EoRs once a week, but you should be meeting with the high-potential ones regularly enough that they know their careers are being considered. Further, your EoRs can provide valuable feedback on how your direct reports are doing as managers. You must also make yourself approachable and available to any EoRs who want career development advice, mentoring, or to discuss a situation where they feel their manager hasn't treated them fairly.

On the other side, if you want some career guidance but your MoR doesn't seem to know you exist, let your manager know and ask for help in approaching your MoR to let him or her know your hopes and expectations... don't wait to be sought out.

And yes, if you are a CEO or President, you have MoR accountabilities too!

(See also *Three-tier units*, page 82.)

In an accountability-based company...

- MoRs do the following:
    - make sure their direct reports exercise the managerial leadership practices described on page 52.
    - establish EoR work levels and placement in compensation bands.
    - develop the talent pool of EoRs (includes mentoring and career planning).
    - assess EoRs' current and future potential capability (see *Capability*, page 8).
    - plan succession for roles one level down.
    - ensure EoRs are treated fairly and equitably across the organization.
    - finalize EoRs' placement in/removal from role and, when appropriate, removal from the organization.
    - ensure EoR's cross-boundary relationships are defined and effective.

- Employees feel comfortable going to their MoR for career planning.

- Employees can approach their MoR, without fear of retribution, if they have a problem with their manager that best efforts have failed to resolve.

"The world is so empty if one thinks only of mountains, rivers, and cities, but to know that there is someone who, though distant, thinks and feels with us—this makes the earth for us an inhabited garden." (Johann Wolfgang von Goethe, German dramatist, novelist, poet, and scientist, 1749–1832)

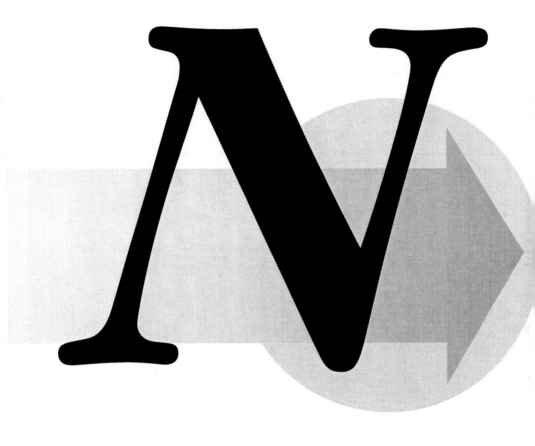

N is for no surprises, no excuses

Surprise (v):   to take unawares; to strike with wonder or amazement especially because unexpected

Excuse (n):   an expression of regret for failure to do something

The "early warning system" is a cornerstone of accountability-based management. It means that direct reports keep their manager appropriately informed about the progress of tasks, and let their manager know immediately if they sense they will meet their goal either ahead of or behind the scheduled time, or if resources will be consumed at a greater or lesser rate than planned. Early warning allows managers to consider other things that will be affected by this change, inform their own manager, and modify their plans accordingly. But this doesn't mean managers need to be breathing down their direct reports' necks as they do their work. It does mean managers need to set up the right processes and environment so their direct reports feel comfortable telling them how things are going.

In an accountability-based company...

- Managers know how direct reports are progressing with their work without it feeling like constant supervision.

- There is no blame attached to not meeting a goal, as long as your manager finds out about it early enough to make alternative plans.

- "I didn't know" is not an acceptable excuse for a manager to give.

- There's no such thing as good news or bad news. It's just news.

"It is wise to direct your anger towards problems—not people; to focus your energies on answers—not excuses." (William Arthur Ward, American, author, pastor, and teacher, 1921–1994)

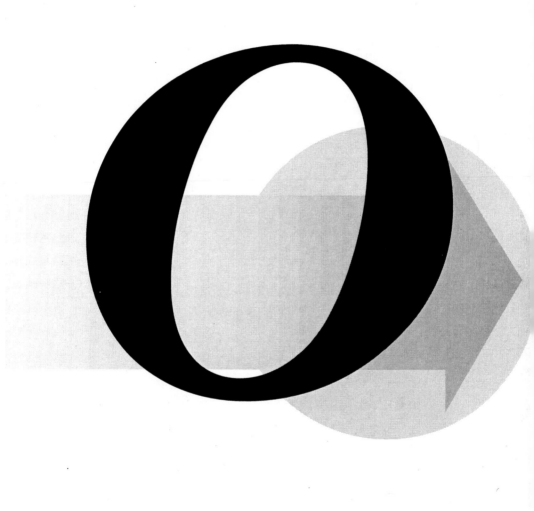

O is for output

Output (n):   mental or artistic production; the amount produced by a person in a given time

Output is what you do or produce. It can be something concrete, like a departmental budget, or something abstract like customer service. Under accountability-based principles, there are five types of output:

1. Direct output (DO)—you produce it yourself.

2. Aided direct output (ADO)—someone helps you produce it.

3. Direct output support (DOS)—you help someone produce it.

4. Delegated direct output (DDO)—you ask someone else to produce it, but you're still accountable for it.

5. Policy controlled direct output (PCDO)—you produce it yourself, but have to get approval—e.g. from Legal or Communications—before you send it out anywhere.

For most people this is just an interesting (or not) snippet of information. It's useful when designing an organization because it helps identify who is truly accountable for what work, which roles need to be grouped together, and who needs to have the authority to ask for what across boundaries. For example, if you always need input from someone to produce your monthly plan, you might have difficulty getting that input in time if the other person is in a different difficulty getting that input in time if the other person is in a different geographic location, reports to a different manager, and has different priorities. One way to resolve this difficulty could be to move the other person closer and have him/her report to the same manager as you, thus making you both members of a collateral team.

In an accountability-based company...

- People know what work is their own direct output and what they delegate.

- Managers accept full accountability for work they've delegated.

- Work is grouped appropriately to facilitate aided direct output and direct output support.

- People understand when sign-off is required on their direct outputs, and where to go for that approval.

"Nothing can be produced out of nothing." (Diogenes Laertius, 3rd century Greek writer)

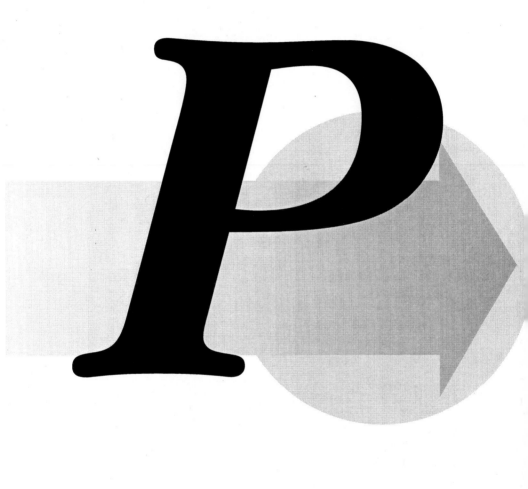

P is for performance

Performance (n):   the execution of an action; the fulfillment of a claim, promise, or request

Surveys indicate that one of the most important elements of job satisfaction is for people to understand the performance measurement system and how they're doing. This requires more than an annual performance review: frequent and timely feedback on how people are performing ensures they stay on track, and surfaces problems early. It doesn't need to be a lengthy one-on-one meeting: managers can recognize good performance (or the lack of it) with an informal verbal comment.

Performance is not just about producing required outputs within the expected timeframe. Managers need to consider how people achieved their results (what were their behaviours) and under what conditions. For example, someone who achieved only 60% of plan because of unexpected market conditions over which he/she had no control might have performed better during the year than someone who achieved 110% of plan because some business was handed to him/her on a plate.

Performance measurement is not objective, nor can it be made to be. It's a manager's judgment, and a manager's work involves making this type of judgment. If a manager consistently makes poor judgments about direct reports, that's an issue for the MoR!

In an accountability-based company...

- People understand the performance management system.

- Managers provide frequent and timely feedback to their direct reports, then provide coaching to make up any shortfalls.

- Performance evaluation is based not just on what is achieved, but on how and under what conditions.

- Employees can appeal to their MoR, without fear of retribution, if they feel unfairly evaluated.

"People forget how fast you did a job—but they remember how well you did it."
(Howard Newton, American advertising executive, 1903–1951)

P is also for personal effectiveness

Effective (n): producing a decided, decisive, or desired effect; readiness for service or action

Personal (adj): of, relating to, or affecting a person; done in person without the intervention of another

Personal effectiveness is how well someone applies him or herself to the tasks in a role. It's one of the things a manager judges when evaluating a direct report's performance: this is the "how" part of goal achievement. However, the manager does not make this judgment in isolation. The manager-once-removed ensures fairness and equity by discussing such judgments with his or her own direct report team, as well as with other managers-once-removed.

In an accountability-based company...

- Everyone can be counted on to do their best.

- Personal effectiveness is not measured by complicated points scales: it's a manager's judgment.

- Managers-once-removed meet with their own direct reports to discuss and compare the performance of employees-once-removed within the three-tier unit (see page 82).

- Groups of managers-once-removed meet regularly to discuss and compare the performance of employees-once-removed and ensure managers across the organization are passing fair judgments.

"An empowered organization is one in which individuals have the knowledge, skill, desire, and opportunity to personally succeed in a way that leads to collective organizational success." (Stephen R. Covey, American author and consultant, 1932–)

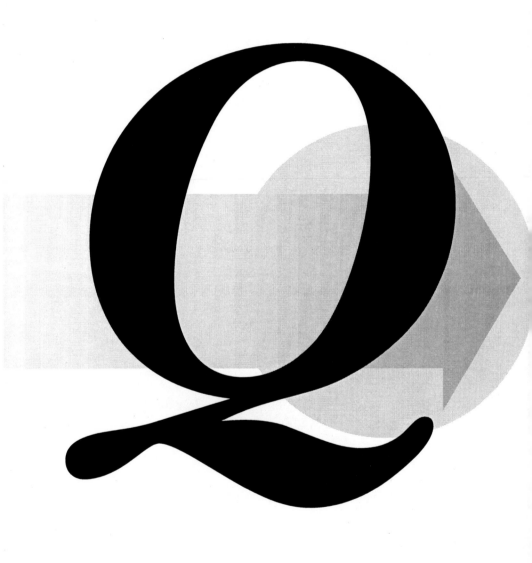

Q is for QQTR

Quantity (n):	an indefinite amount or number; a determinate or estimated amount
Quality (n):	peculiar and essential character
Time (n):	the measured or measurable period during which an action, process, or condition exists or continues
Resources (n):	a source of supply or support; an available means

QQTRs are the elements of a task—the "what by when, and with what." When a manager asks for something to be done, it's important for both the manager and the direct report to understand these elements:

Quantity	How much, how many
Quality	How well it should be done, and any special criteria or conditions to be met
Time	When it needs to be completed
Resources	What people, money, authorities are available

Most managers don't assign work clearly. They usually know when and how they want things to be done, but often forget to be specific. Since many direct reports feel they shouldn't ask too many questions, just get the job done, it's not surprising that they don't always meet their manager's expectations. If you're a manager, be aware of these elements and make them as specific as possible when delegating work.

When your manager assigns a task using QQTR, you need to consider if it's feasible or not. If it's feasible, be clear that you accept the task. If not, let your manager know immediately so the two of you can negotiate. For example,

Sue : Bob, I'd like you analyze our customer satisfaction survey results.

Bob: When do you want this to be done?

Sue: Oh, by next Monday.

Bob: I can do it by next Monday, but the monthly budget won't get done as well. Which would you prefer?

Sue: I need both. What if I ask Sunil to help you with the budget?

Bob: Yes, that will work. I can do it by Monday.

Remember that if, while a task is being carried out, any one of the QQTR elements changes, it affects the others. Use the early warning system: let your manager know immediately so you can renegotiate and your manager can plan accordingly.

In an accountability-based company...

- Managers always make sure their direct reports understand the QQTRs of delegated work.

- People feel comfortable questioning and negotiating QQTRs with their manager.

- Managers and direct reports renegotiate QQTRs when situations change.

"Quality is never an accident; it is always the result of high intention, sincere effort, intelligent direction and skilful execution; it represents the wise choice of many alternatives." (William A. Foster)

R is for responsibility

Responsible (adj):   able to choose for oneself between right and wrong

Accountability and responsibility are not the same thing: accountability is the obligation to answer for an action, while responsibility is a felt obligation to act within the values of an organization. For example, if a customer complains to someone who is not accountable for handling complaints, the responsible thing for that person to do is see that the complaint goes to the right place for resolution. It may be true, but is not helpful, to say "Sorry, that's not my job."

In an accountability-based company...

- Employees feel a shared sense of responsibility to make the company the best it can be.

- Employees ensure whatever actions they take, they do not intentionally harm any other employees.

"I believe that every right implies a responsibility; every opportunity an obligation; every possession a duty." (John D. Rockefeller, Jr., American philanthropist, 1874–1960)

R is also for rewards and recognition

Reward (n):   something that is given in return for good or evil done or received and especially that is offered or given for some service or attainment

Recognition (n):   special notice or attention

People need to know how well they're doing, and they appreciate recognition for doing a good job. Compensation is one way to recognize people, but recognition over and above compensation lets people know their contribution is truly appreciated and inspires people to do their best.

It is a manager's job to provide rewards and recognition. Unfortunately, many managers simply expect excellent work and forget to let people know when they are meeting these expectations. Instead, they tend to focus on what goes wrong or praise only exceptional work.

Recognition doesn't have to be in the form of bonuses or other cash rewards. Something as simple as a "thank you" e-mail from the CEO to someone further down in the organization might be all that's needed when someone has done an excellent job. When developing a rewards and recognition program, managers need to work with employees to find out what they really value as a reward and appreciate as recognition.

In an accountability-based company...

- Managers ensure people feel appreciated for doing good work.

- Employees receive regular feedback on how they are doing.

- Rewards and recognition are in a form that employees truly value.

- Managers have sufficient authority to provide appropriate rewards.

"In the arena of human life the honours and rewards fall to those who show their good qualities in action." (Aristotle, Greek philosopher, scientist, and physician, 384–322 BC)

And R is for role-person fit

Role (n):   a character assigned or assumed

Fit (v):   to be suitable for or to harmonize with

Role-person fit is how well a person's information processing capability (see page 37), knowledge and skills, valuing of the work, and behaviour match what is required in a role:

How well a person fits a role is a function of

| Information processing capability (IPC) | + | Knowledge and skills (K/S) | + | Valuing the work (V) | + | Required behaviour (RB) |

Of these only information processing capability (IPC), which is inherent and develops with time, cannot be improved through training and coaching. Since someone with a lower level of IPC than is required by a role is almost guaranteed to fail, managers and managers-once-removed need to work together to ensure they select people with the right information processing capability for particular roles.

There are some people who will never value a particular type of work and are therefore not a good fit for a role—for example, a highly skilled technical individual contributor who does not have any interest in managing people should not be placed in a managerial role "because that's the only way we can pay you what you're worth." In most cases, however, people can work with their manager to develop knowledge and skills, to learn how to value the work, and to understand how to demonstrate required behaviour (behaviour that is in line with company values).

If someone who is over-qualified is placed in a role, he or she may start to invent work that better matches his/her IPC and skills/knowledge. It may be useful work, or it may be perceived as mischief. The person will likely also feel underpaid. It's important for managers to address the issue of role-person fit, and not to artificially inflate the role's pay or boundaries to accommodate an over-qualified candidate.

Sometimes people take roles for which they are over-qualified (have greater IPC than is required) because they do something else outside of work where they use their full capability—for example, volunteer work or supporting a spouse's business—and do not want additional challenge. This is workable, as long as the person, the manager, and the manager-once-removed are aware of the situation, are clear that the role expectations must still be met, and do not allow the role (or the pay) to grow to match the person's capability.

In an accountability-based company…

- People have the right information processing capability, knowledge, and skills to perform effectively in their role.

- People value their own and others' work, and are not required to do work they don't value just so they can be paid fairly.

- People demonstrate appropriate behaviour in their role.

- People are given sufficient opportunities to develop role-related skills and knowledge.

- Employees can appeal to their manager-once-removed if their manager does not demonstrate appropriate managerial behaviour.

"Anyone who is capable of getting themselves made President should on no account be allowed to do the job." (Douglas Adams, English humorist and science fiction novelist, 1952–2001)

S is for service giving and getting

Service (n): contribution to the welfare of others

Within any organization there are usually people who need to get a service from others who work for a different manager. For example, Human Resources provides services in the form of help with recruitment and hiring to people across an organization; Information Technology provides hardware, software, and consulting services. If technology is outsourced, an outside company provides these services, although someone within the company must still be accountable for the quality of the services provided. Service giving and getting is the most widespread form of cross-boundary relationship (see *Cross-boundary relationships*, page 98). People can run into problems if it is not clear who has what authority over whom, and what obligations each party has to the other.

If the service giver and the service receiver are in the same organization, it should be easy for the two parties to meet and agree on required service levels and authorities. In case of disagreement, the respective managers and managers-once-removed can help clarify what's needed. If a service is outsourced, however, there is less control and potentially poorer understanding. It's harder work, but still possible for those involved to be very clear about expectations, and what the roles and authorities are. Often a formal Service Level Agreement can specify what's required on both sides.

In an accountability-based company...

- Work is grouped appropriately to minimize cross-functional friction.

- Service-getters and service-givers meet regularly to clarify needs and expectations.

- Service-getters

    - clearly describe their expectations and the reasons behind them.

    - understand the degree of authority they have with service-givers.

    - escalate problems to their respective managers only if they can't resolve them themselves.

- Service-givers

  - understand what they must provide, by when, to what quality, and why.

  - understand the degree of authority a service-getter has.

  - advise service-getters in plenty of time if they are unable to meet their commitments.

  - escalate problems to their respective managers only if they can't resolve them themselves.

- If work is outsourced, a full-time company employee is still held accountable for the quality, quantity, and timeliness of that outsourced work.

"The service you do for others is the rent you pay for the time you spend on earth." (Mohammed Ali, Macedonian governor and later viceroy of Egypt, c.1769–1849)

S is also for skills

Skill (n):   the ability to use one's knowledge effectively and readily in execution or performance; dexterity or coordination especially in the execution of learned physical tasks; a learned power of doing something competently; a developed aptitude or ability

Along with knowledge, skills are an element of the role-person fit formula (a person's suitability for a particular role—see page 72). If a role candidate (or incumbent) is lacking in skills, it is relatively easy to resolve the issue with coaching, training, or work experience. Managers need to be watching for skill deficiencies, coaching where appropriate, and ensuring appropriate training is provided.

In an accountability-based company...

- People have, or can easily obtain, the skills they need to meet their accountabilities.

- Managers are aware of skill gaps and take actions to close them.

- People are comfortable requesting training if they feel they need it.

"A smooth sea never made a skilled mariner." (English proverb)

And S is for span of control

Span (n):   an extent, stretch, reach, or spread between two limits

Control (n):   power or authority to guide or manage

Span of control is the number of direct reports that a manager has. The term would probably be better named "span of support," since it really relates to how a manager can best support his/her team members. A manager with too many direct reports cannot provide adequate coaching, recognition, and feedback to his/her team members. Too few direct reports and a manager will have to "dip down" and do extra work that distracts him or her from important managerial work.

There is no precise number that represents the "right" span of control, but there are principles to help establish what is best for a particular role. The manager must be able to

- effectively judge the personal effectiveness of each direct report.

- provide the required coaching and performance feedback to each direct report.

- effectively perform his/her own work.

The following factors affect the size of a manager's span of control:

- The similarity of direct reports' work
  (more similar = more direct reports possible).

- The complexity of direct reports' work
  (more complex = fewer direct reports possible).

- Direct reports' geographic location
  (more widespread = fewer direct reports possible).

- Direct reports capability, knowledge, and skills
  (greater levels = more direct reports possible).

In an accountability-based company…

- Each manager has the right span of control to effectively carry out his/her managerial leadership practices.

- Each manager is able to do his/her own work and is not required to "dip down" to fill in for missing roles.

"There is no safety in numbers, or in anything else." (James Thurber, American author, cartoonist, humorist, and satirist, 1894–1961)

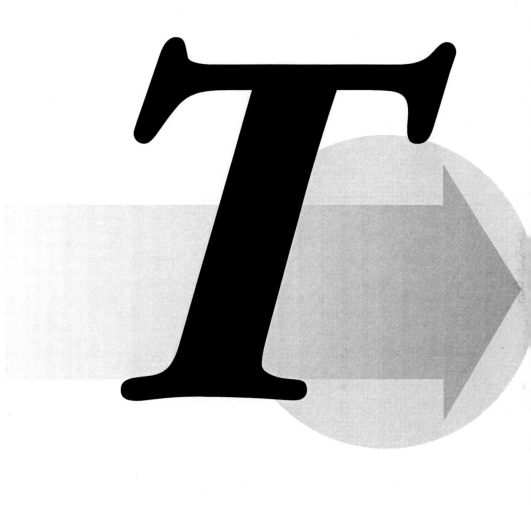

T is for three-tier units

Tier (n):   two or more rows, levels, or ranks arranged one
above another

A three-tier unit is made up of a manager-once-removed, all
his/her direct reports, and all their direct reports.

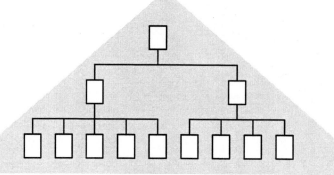

This three-tier unit is a foundation of accountability-based
management. It is sometimes called a mutual recognition unit, on
the premise that everyone in the unit should at least be able to
recognize everyone else. Research and practical application
indicate that, for this reason, a three-tier unit starts to break down
at around 250 people.

The most important aspect of three-tier management is that it
puts in place a manager-once-removed for all employees—
someone those employees can go to for career advice and
mentoring, or if they feel unfairly treated by their manager, and
someone who makes sure managers carry out their required
managerial leadership practices. (See also *Manager-once-removed*,
page 53 and *Manager*, page 52.)

In an accountability-based company...

- People understand the concept of three tiers.

- Three-tier meetings take place from time to time.

- Managers-once-removed exercise their unique accountabilities to ensure fairness and equity across the unit.

- Groups of managers-once-removed meet to discuss career opportunities for their employees-once-removed in other three-tier units.

- At a minimum, managers-once-removed know the faces of all people in their three-tier unit.

"If you remember my name, you pay me a subtle compliment; you indicate that I have made an impression on you. Remember my name and you add to my feeling of importance." (Dale Carnegie, American writer and public speaker, 1888–1955)

T is also for timespan of discretion

Span (n):   an extent, stretch, reach, or spread between two limits; a
                        limited space (as of time)

Discretion (n):   ability to make responsible decisions; individual choice or
                        judgment; power of free decision or latitude of choice within
                        certain legal bounds

The timespan of discretion is the length of time a manager grants a
direct report to complete a task. During this time the direct report
must have the necessary resources (which includes appropriate
authority to make whatever decisions are needed). The direct report
may "check in" with the manager, keep the manager advised of
progress, discuss issues, and obtain advice, but is accountable for
getting the task done.

The timespan of discretion of the longest task in a role determines
the level (complexity) of work someone is doing. A longer timespan
is likely to involve more variables and unknowns, and requires the
ability to juggle shorter tasks against the longer one so all work is
completed at the right time and to quality standards (see also *Level of
work complexity*, page 48). Someone who is given a task with a longer
timespan of discretion than he/she can handle will tend to focus on
the shorter-term tasks and neglect the longer one until it is too late to
successfully complete it. Conversely, someone who is given tasks
with very short timespans of discretion but who is capable of
handling longer ones will become frustrated and bored, and may start
to invent tasks with a timespan that matches their own capability.

In an accountability-based company...

- Managers delegate work with an appropriate timespan of
  discretion for their direct reports.

- Managers provide resources for direct reports to do the work,
  and do not interfere (but provide advice if asked).

- Managers watch for signs that their direct reports are capable of
  handling tasks within the designated timespan of discretion, and
  make adjustments as necessary (breaking larger tasks down into
  smaller chunks for those who struggle, or discussing with a
  person's MoR if a person is over-capable and needs to be given
  some developmental opportunities).

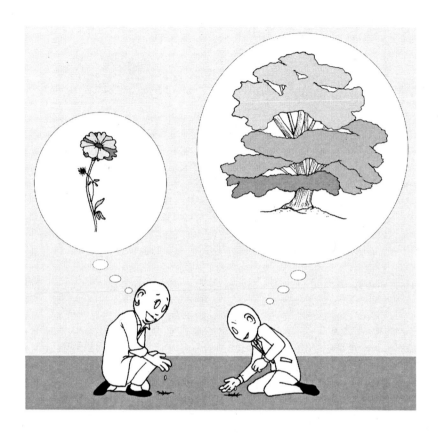

"It takes twenty years to make an overnight success." (Eddie Cantor, American comedian and singer, 1892–1964)

And T is for trust

Trust (n):   assured reliance on the character, ability, strength, or truth of someone or something

An accountability-based workplace is built on trust and the premise that people in the workplace can be sure no-one else in the workplace will intentionally do them harm. Managers and managers-once-removed need to promote trust by being fair and consistent. All employees need to promote trust by being honest in their conversations and sticking to commitments, or letting people know early if they can no longer do so.

In an accountability-based company...

- People do not intentionally do harm to each other.

- People trust others to do their work to the best of their ability.

- People trust their manager to treat them fairly and equitably.

- People trust their manager-once-removed to look out for their career interests.

- People make realistic commitments, and manage those commitments impeccably.

"Trust is the lubrication that makes it possible for organizations to work."
(Warren G. Bennis, American psychologist, management educator, and consultant, 1925–)

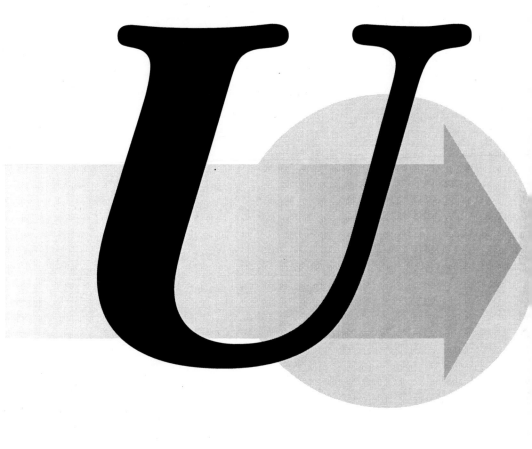

U is for under-performance

Performance (n):   the execution of an action; something accomplished

Under (adj):   lower than usual, proper, or desired in amount, quality, or degree

Someone who is under-performing is someone who is not achieving their goals or meeting his/her manager's expectations. It may be because the person is not the right one for the role: perhaps he/she finds the work too complex, does not have the skills and knowledge, or does not value the work. There may be other environmental factors that prevent the person from being successful. Whatever the reason, the individual involved usually knows that he/she is no longer on track and is accountable to tell his/her manager (without fear of reprisal), and the manager is accountable to know how that individual is performing and provide coaching at the right time to help the person improve. If, for some reason, the person cannot improve, the manager is also accountable to discuss the situation with the person's manager-once-removed and initiate removal from role. This doesn't necessarily mean firing the person, but it does mean making all possible efforts to find a better role fit.

In an accountability-based company...

- All efforts are made to place people in roles where they can be successful.

- People feel comfortable approaching their manager to discuss factors that prevent them from being successful.

- Managers are aware of how their direct reports are performing, and discuss performance issues promptly.

- Managers initiate removal from a role if a direct report is the wrong person for the job.

"Never promise more than you can perform." (Publilius Syrus, Roman writer of mimes, circa 100 BC)

V is for values

Value (n):   something (as a principle or quality) intrinsically valuable
or desirable

In accountability-based management terms, values are the norms and boundaries that guide how role holders act. Some commonly stated values are mutual trust, openness, honesty, individual recognition, and customer responsiveness. There could be many more.

Since values are personal, no company has the right to impose values on its employees, nor to even ask what its employees' values are. For a successful relationship, employees do not need to personally share the company's stated values, but they do need to be able to support them and behave appropriately to demonstrate that support. In other words, the values describe boundaries within which employees must behave, and allow people (from the front line right up to the leader of the organization) to be called to account for not doing so. As an example, a company may expect its employees to demonstrate the following in support of its values:

- Commitment

- Integrity

- Cooperation

- Reliability

- Initiative

- Personal effectiveness

The requirement to demonstrate these should be made clear when employees are hired, and there should be consequences applied to anyone who doesn't demonstrate them, otherwise it becomes clear that the company's values are something other than what is stated.

It is not a one-way street. Employees who agree to support company values have the right to expect certain things from the company in return. Those things are

- a clearly defined role.
- fulfilling work.
- authority to act.
- a competent manager.
- the opportunity to participate.
- fair treatment.

In an accountability-based company...

- Values are explicitly stated.
- Employee behaviour reflects the company's values.
- People (at any level) can call each other to account for not behaving within the stated values.
- There are consequences for not behaving in ways that support company values.

"It is a good idea to be ambitious, to have goals, to want to be good at what you do, but it is a terrible mistake to let drive and ambition get in the way of treating people with kindness and decency." (Robert Solow, American economist, 1924–)

W is for work

Work (n):   activity in which one exerts strength or faculties to do or perform something; sustained physical or mental effort to overcome obstacles and achieve an objective or result

For people, work is a thinking process that involves using judgment and making decisions to achieve a result or *output*. Doing work always involves making decisions on how best to balance pace (how quickly something must be done) against quality (how well). Work becomes more complex if you have to balance one task against others, and if there are more variables or unknown factors to deal with (see also *Information processing capability*, page 37 and *Level of work complexity*, page 48).

For an organization, work is what goes on to support the customer or to support the company itself. Work can be divided into the following categories:

- Mainstream—work that directly supports and satisfies customer needs (selling, marketing, provisioning, development).

- Resource sustainment—providing services and support to ensure effective stewardship of resources (financial, human, material).

- Resource enhancement—significantly changing or improving how mainstream business work is carried out.

- Staff specialist—providing specialty advice to business unit heads and managers.

In an accountability-based company...

- People understand that there are different levels of work complexity, and that all levels are equally important.

- People have the right capability to perform the work in their role.

- Work is effectively grouped to meet the organization's mandate while minimizing duplication, cross-functional friction, and the cost/effort of coordination.

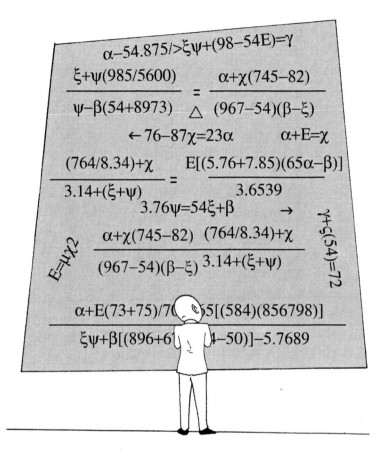

"I think and think for months and years. Ninety-nine times the conclusion is false. The hundredth time I am right." (Albert Einstein, German-born mathematical physicist, 1879–1955)

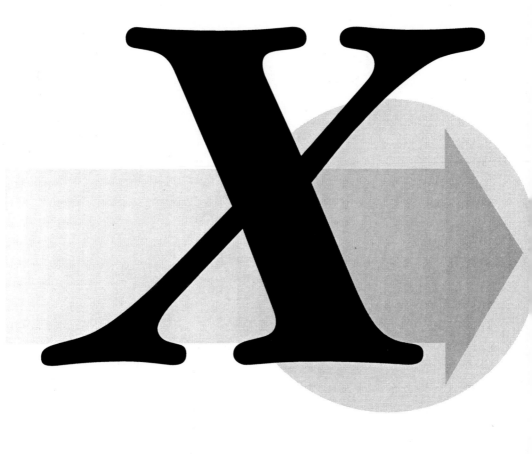

X is for cross-boundary relationships

Cross (Adj):   Lying across or athwart, mutually opposed, involving mutual interchange

Boundary (n):   Something (as a line, point, or plane) that indicates or fixes a limit or extent

Relationship (n):   The state of being related or interrelated; a state of affairs existing between those having relations or dealings

Cross-boundary relationships are those where, in order to do your own work, you need to work with someone else who has a different manager. Unless these relationships are clearly defined and the people involved understand what they can expect of each other (and why) it's all too easy to point fingers and build resentment. As a result, necessary work does not get done well (or at all), and results are compromised.

It is a manager's accountability to define required cross-boundary relationships and authorities for his/her team members. The manager-once-removed is accountable to approve the relationships and deal with any escalated problems. Defining the relationship and required authority means determining if the purpose is to

- get or give a service.

- provide advice.

- coordinate existing work and processes.

- monitor for adherence to policies and practices, and for any impacts on work in other areas.

- audit to ensure adherence to policies, mandated practices, and legislation.

- prescribe a specific course of action that others must follow (without first checking with their own manager).

In an accountability-based company...

- Cross-boundary relationships are clearly defined.

- People understand what is expected of them, and what authority they have across boundaries.

- People know what to do and who to go to if efforts to resolve cross-boundary issues directly fail, and there is no blame attached to escalation. Instead, these situations are treated as problems to solve.

"Assumptions are the termites of relationships." (Henry Winkler, American television actor, 1945–)

Y is for you

You (pron):   the one or ones being addressed

Whether you're an employee, a manager, a manager-once-removed, or an individual contributor, and whatever your role's level of work complexity, you play an important part in the success of your organization. Remember that in return for providing meaningful work and fair pay, the accountability-based organization expects you to do your best at all times. You can help promote an atmosphere of trust by ensuring no surprises (for your manager or your direct reports), making clear commitments and sticking to them, being fair and equitable in your dealings with others, and generally operating in a spirit of cooperation and teamwork.

In an accountability-based company…

- It's well known that people provide the means of achieving the organization's goals.

- Employees, at all levels, do their best at all times.

- People treat others fairly, and with honesty and respect.

- People at all levels are valued for their unique contribution.

"The roots of true achievement lie in the will to become the best that you can become." (Harold Taylor, British architect, 1895–1919)

Z is for ze glossary and ze end

A quick reference for some of the terms that come up regularly in this book:

Employee-once-removed (EoR)	A direct report of your direct report; an employee two levels down.
Gap	A situation where a person does not have a manager performing work at the next highest level of complexity.
Individual contributor	A person who provides specialized knowledge or skills, usually without direct reports.
IPC	Information processing capability—a person's ability to make plans and decisions based on a number of different pieces of information. The more variables involved, the more complex the thinking involved.
Jam-up	A situation where a manager and direct report are both performing the same work.
Manager-once-removed (MoR)	Your manager's manager, with unique accountabilities regarding your fair treatment and career development.
Output	Something you produce: the end result of a task.
Role-person fit or role fit	How well a person's information processing capability, knowledge/skills, valuing of the work, and behaviours match those required by a role.
Timespan (of discretion)	The length of time a manager grants a direct report to carry out a particular task.
Level of work	A band of work of a particular complexity. The timespan of discretion of a role's tasks determine its level of work.

Questions or comments?

COREinternational inc
366 Adelaide Street West, Suite 606
Toronto, ON M5V 1R9 Canada

(416) 977-2673/(800) 361-5282

www.coreinternational.com

info@coreinternational.com